Indian
COOKING
Cook Book

recipes as told to,
and translated by,
Bruce Carlson

Beth Waljasper   In-Black-Water Jobe   Jeb Larkin
Running Hair   Robert Stilwell   Many Days Eid

Table of Contents

Foreward

Bruce Carlson, in the INDIAN COOKING COOK BOOK, has managed to walk a fine line between opposing goals.

He has provided us with authentic Indian recipes, yet has made them usable to a cook in this day of entirely different ingredients and methods of cooking.

Professor Phil Hey
Briar Cliff College
Sioux City, Iowa

Dedicated

to the almost inaudible sound of the wind

as it passes through the buffalo grass ...

and to the smell of the dust to the hunter

as his paint bears him out of this time...

to the time of the buffalo grass.

Preface

The reader will find, in this book, recipes that come to use from the lodges and campfires of the Lakota, the Chippewa, the Cherokee, the Ottowa, and the Cree.

The author of this cookbook has translated the ingredients, methods of measurement, and the practices of those people to modern times and to modern kitchens.

The taste and the feel of the prairie remains.

Vegetables

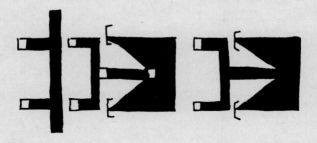

Wild Mustard

The greens can be eaten raw or cooked like spinach. Add onion stems chopped into short pieces before cooking. Melted fat over the greens helps the flavor.

Squash or Pumpkin

Cut in half, take out seeds. Section into chunks, add water and maple sugar. Cookover low heat so it can be smashed with a fork.

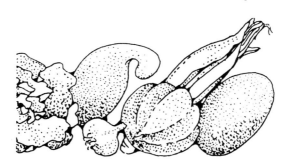

Wild Celery

Leaves can be cooked as any other vegetable.

Dried Corn Soup

Dry corn on cob, then remove. Boil, using at least twice as much water, as corn.

Succotash

Corn and beans are boiled together with a little fat. Use no more water than that needed to just cover the corn and beans.

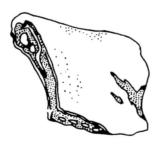

Squash or Pumpkin

Cut hole in top, and take seeds out. Stuff with cooked rice, add water to keep moist, and replace top. Bake at low heat.

Greens

Pick only the tender young ones in the spring. Cook them with water just barley covering them. When well wilted they are ready to eat. Treat like spinach.

Roast Corn

Take off husks and silk. Replace husks, soak in water. Roast in ashes until corn is well steamed to tender.

Cooked Corn

Cut from the cob and cook in a little water and seasoning to taste.

Wood Ferns

Cut fern in the spring when they are still curled up. Trim off any brown parts, put several ounces in a pot, cover with water, and boil. Cut back on the heat, and let simmer until tender. Season with a little ginger or fat.

Squash or Pumpkin

Cut into chunks, scrape off seeds and string. Set by fire to bake, turning for even cooking.

Pumpkin

Cut ripe pumpkin into rings. Peel, dry by fire slowly. Wash and cook. Season as desired.

Plantain

Bring water to a boil, and add the leaves. Treat as one would spinach.

Horsetail

Remove outer layers. Dip the raw shoots in drippings from roasting wild game, briefly hold them over the same fire until lightly smoked.
Can also be eaten raw.

Squash Blossoms

Put the blossoms in boiling water for only about one minute. Dip the blossoms in batter, and deep fry. The best blossoms are those still unopened.

Cattail Sprouts

The sprouts may be havested in early spring. This will be shortly after the snow disappears from the marshes. Try to get the youngest ones. These are the most tender.

Put one inch pieces in a pot, covered with water. Add seasonings. Popular ones have been onions or maple sugar. Ginger is good, too. Simmer just a few minutes until the sprouts are tender.

Cattail sprouts are a lot like asparagus. The same sauces used for asparagus can be used for these delicious sprouts.

Squash and Pumpkin Seeds

Roast seeds in oven, and salt just before serving.

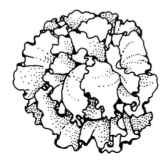

Cabbage

Wilt cabbage in small amount of hot grease. Add some green pepper chunks and cook 'til cabbage turns red. Good with cornbread.

Watercress

Gather in woods. Wash in cool water. Drip hot grease over the cress and add a bit of sweetened vinegar. Or, can be eaten raw with salt and without the grease and vinegar.

Parched Corn

Put hot ashes in a pot, and add corn, stir until brown. Clean off ashes, beat corn in beater. Make soup by stirring large pieces in boiling water. Cook to taste.

Tomato Fritters

2 C. tomatoes that are not
* yet fully ripe*
1/2 tsp. salt

1 C. corn meal

Mix all into tomatoes and fry in a hot pan to brown. Makes 8 fritters.

Ka-Ti-A Potatoes

6 med. potatoes   *pepper to taste*
Walnut sized lump of butter   *fist of flour*
salt   *C. of milk*

Wash, peel, and slice raw potatoes. Should be sliced thin. Put in layer in greased baking dish. Season in layers with salt, pepper, and sprinkle lightly with flour. Scatter with small pieces of butter. Add milk to within one finger of top of potatoes. Bake 1 hr. at 350°.

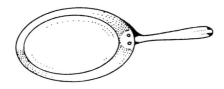

Green Beans with Tomatoes

2 T. butter   *1 T. salt*
2 T. chopped onion   *1 minced garlic clove*
2 T. chopped parsley   *Double handful of sliced beans*
4 med. peeled and chopped tomatoes

In skillet over medium heat, cook onions and garlic in hot butter 'til tender. Add tomatoes and salt, then simmer while covered for 10 minutes. Add beans, cook 'til heated well.

Baked Tomatoes

Wash tomatoes and slice into 2 pieces. Put on baking sheet with cut side up. Sprinkle with butter and grated cheese, salt and pepper. Bake until tender.

Corn In A Husk

Drop ear of corn in husk in hot fat, and fry to golden color. (Aluminum foil can be used instead of husk.)

Eggplant Fritters (or squash)

Put eggplants in salted water (use cold water, and whole egg plants.) Boil 'til can be easily pierced with knife. Peel, mash and season with salt, pepper, and butter. Add a beaten egg and 2 T. flour. Drop by spoon onto hot griddle.

Cattail Roots

These can be treated like potatoes, and eaten raw or cooked.

Cabbage Rolls

1 C. cooked tomatoes
1/2 C. cooked rice
2 tsp. salt
1 lg. head cabbage
1/2 tsp. pepper.

2 T. brown sugar
1 lb. ground venison
   (hamburger can be used)
1 C. milk

Cook rice. Put leaves of cabbage in hot water. Dry them. Mix meat, milk, and seasoning, and rice. Put small rolls of meat in cabbage. Secure with toothpick. Put rolls in kettle and cover with lg. can tomatoes. Cook 2 hrs.

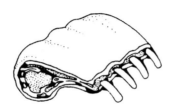

Cattail Fluff

The fluff is added to soups and stews to act as a thickening agent. Or, add it to pancake mix at a rate of about 1/4 C. of fluff to each cup of batter.

Hashed Hominy

2 C. strained hominy
4 beaten eggs
pepper

butter as needed
salt

Brown hominy over medium heat. Add beaten eggs. Season and stir. Serve when hominy is brown.

Maple-Candied Sweet Potatoes

2 1/2 lb. baked sweet potatoes   1/4 tsp. cinnamon
1/2 C. packed brown sugar   1/4 tsp. salt
1/2 C. maple syrup   2 T. butter

This must be done about 1 hour before serving.

Preheat oven to 325°. Put potatoes in greased large shallow casserole. In med. saucepan over med. heat, heat to boiling the rest of the ingredients, stirring now and then. Pour over potatoes. Bake 35 min., beating occasionally with mixture in dish.

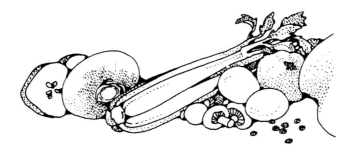

Fritter Batter

1 C. flour   1/2 C. milk
1 1/2 tsp. baking powder   pinch of salt
2 T. sugar   egg

When you fry raw vegetables you must fry in fat hot enough to brown a cube of bread in one minute. Mix above and drop large spoonful in hot grease deep enough to cover. Turn enough to brown fritter all over. The above batter may be used on cubes of fruit rolled in maple candy (powdered), dip batter and fry.

Mixed Vegetables

4 zucchini (about 6-10 in.)	*1 clove garlic*
4 tomatoes	*2 T. olive oil*
4 bell peppers	*3 T. lemon juice*
4 onions	*2 tsp. sugar*
1 eggplant	*salt and pepper*

Slice peeled zucchini, tomatoes, onion and eggplant. Seed and quarter peppers, mince garlic. Heat oil. Add vegetables, and season in layers. Cook at low heat for 1 hr. Sir as needed. Serve hot or cold.

Fried Sweet Potatoes

Peel and cut sweet potatoes. Fry in skillet in fat, while turning frequently. Add 3-4 tsp. sugar and 3/4 C. milk when potatoes are almost fried. Simmer 'til done.

Tomato Fritters

2 C. tomatoes	*salt*
1 C. cornmeal	*pepper*

Mix above into tomatoes. Shape into pones, and fry to brown in hot grease.

Browned Carrots

2 slightly beaten eggs
1 doz. med. cooked carrots
2 C. crushed corn (can sub.
  corn flakes)
1/4 C. brown sugar

1 T. lemon juice
2 T. milk
1/4 C. butter

Mix eggs and milk. Dip carrots in and then into the corn. Brown in butter. Sprinkle with brown sugar and lemon juice.

Turnips

Peel and cook in salted water 'til tender. Drain, add walnut-sized lump of butter, 1 T. flour, a pinch of salt and pepper to taste. Cook with a little milk or cream until thickened.

Fried Okras (or green tomatoes)

4 C. okra cut crosswise
1 C. cornmeal
bacon drippings

salt
pepper

Tumble okra with cornmeal. Season with salt and pepper. Saute in skillet with 4 tablespoons of bacon drippings. Cook 10-15 min.

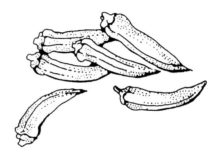

Sweet & Sour Red Cabbage

3 slices of bacon that have been
  diced and dried
6 C. shredded red cabbage
3 cloves
salt
pepper

1/4 C. brown sugar
pinch cinnamon
3 T. vinegar
2 peeled and sliced apples
1 C. boiling water

Fry cabbage with salt and pepper, cloves, and apples. Add water. Cover and cook at low heat for 15 min. Blend in flour, cinnamon, sugar, and vinegar. Add cabbage. Heat to thick, add bacon and serve while still hot.

Corn Pudding

2 C. fresh corn
3 eggs slightly beaten
2 tsp. sugar
2 C. milk

2 T. butter
1 1/2 tsp. salt
pinch pepper

Add corn, sugar, salt, and pepper. Add eggs then, and mix. Heat butter and milk, then add that to corn. Bake 325° 1 hr. or 'til knife comes out clean.

Corn Meal

1 C. cream syle corn
1/3 C. cooking oil
2 eggs, well beaten
1 onion

1 C. self rising white meal
1/2 C. sweet milk
1 C. cheese
1 banana pepper

Dice onion, cheese, pepper and mix the rest of above. Season to taste. Bake at 375° 35min. Cool and slice.

Squash Fluff

1 1/2 C. milk
2 eggs
2 C. cooked squash

1 T. brown sugar
salt
pepper

Mash squash, add milk, sugar, seasoning and egg yolk. Beat whites, and fold in. Put in baking dish. Bake at 350° to taste.

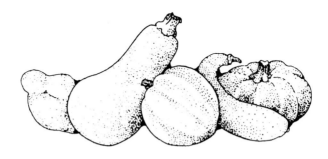

Creamed Potatoes

2 C. diced potatoes
1 1/2 T. butter
1 1/2 T. flour

1 tsp. salt/pepper mix
1 C. milk

Cook potatoes in boiled salted water until they are tender. Melt butter and blend in the flour, salt and pepper. Gradually stir in milk and cook over low heat until thick. Keep well stirred. Add the drained and hot diced potatoes to the sauce.

Creases

Pick the creases when they are tender. Wash. Boil, and then fry in grease.

Leather Breeches

Break beans and string on thread, hang in sun to dry. Par-boil, wash, remove from string. Cook with salt or other seasoning until done.

Dried Cabbage

Cut head of cabbage in fourths. Store in dry place through the winter. When ready to eat it, par-boil it, wash, and cook again with seasoning of choice.

Corn Pudding

1 doz. ears of sweet corn   *2 T. flour*
1 1/2 T. sugar   *1 T. butter*
1 qt. milk   *3 eggs*
salt to taste

Grate corn and mix in milk. Work flour and butter 'til creamy. Beat sugar and egg yolks. Add beaten whites. Put into the corn and milk mix. Salt to taste. Bake. Can be sweetened with sugar or cream.

Ramps

Ramps are of the lily family. Fry them with bacon or ham and eggs.

Cornmeal Potatoes

Dice raw potato, roll in cornmeal, season with salt to taste. Also add pepper to taste. Fry in hot grease.

Aspen Bark

Strip off bark, and remove the soft inner bark. This soft part is sweet.

Mushrooms

Gather safe mushrooms. Wash. Par-broil, and wash again. Throw away slimy part, and fry in grease. Add butter. Do not gather your own mushrooms unless you know mushrooms well. Many mushrooms are poisonous.

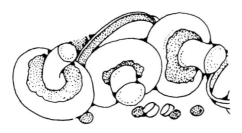

Artichokes

Gather from woods, wash and eat. Salt improves flavor.

Dandelion Greens

Dandelions can be used until they bloom. Pick over the dandelions, and wash in salt water. Rinse several times. Put in boiling water, with piece of salt pork. Boil 1 hr. Drain well, add salt and boil another 2 hr. When done drain well.

Succotash

1 pt. of cooked green beans   *1 pt. tomatoes*
1 pt. cooked off-cob corn   *meat drippings*

Cook all above together, and add, when half cooked, a little minced onion, salt and pepper.

Wild Rice Stew

1 C. wild rice
2 lb. stew meat
1 onion chopped
1 C. celery, chopped
4 oz. mushrooms (edible)

1 can cream of mushroom
  soup
1/2 C. green pepper, chopped
1/8 lb. butter

Simmer the wild rice in water until the kernels flower out. Cut the meat into bite-size pieces, brown in a hot skillet.

Saute onion, celery, and green pepper in butter over low heat until onions are clear (3-4 min.).

Use a greased and covered baking dish. Put all ingredients in the dish, and mix well. Cover and bake 2 hours at 350°. Add water if necessary to prevent it from becoming too dry.

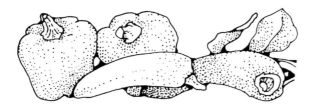

Scalloped Cabbage

1 med. head shredded cabbage
2 C. med. white sauce

1 C. grated cheese

Cook cabbage for 5 min. in covered pan in an inch of boiling water with 1 tsp. salt. The liquid can be used for white sauce. Put cabbage in baking dish and pour sauce over it. Top with cheese, bake 20 min. at 375°.

Fire Weed

Cut the young sprouts into sections and boil them until tender. Season to taste and eat.

Drinks

Trail Catnip Tea

Add a handful of fresh leaves to a pot of boiling water, reduce heat and let simmer about 15 min.

Cornmeal Gravy

Fry enough meat to get grease enough to cover 1/2 C. of cornmeal. Salt to taste. Brown meal in grease to light brown. Add 2 1/2 C. milk, stir and boil to thick. Serve hot over bread.

Fried Bread

Make a soft dough from 1 C. flour, 1 tsp. baking powder, pinch of salt, and a little grease. Add enough milk to mix. Cut this together. Drop by spoonfuls into hot grease and let fry until brown and crisp. Serve hot.

Chestnut Bread

Peel a pound of chestnuts. Remove the inside skin. Mix with enough cornmeal to stick together. Add boiling water to make dough. Wrap in shucks, and bake.

Pine Needle Tea

Make a bundle of about two dozen Norway or White Pine needles. New green needles in summer work the best. Cut off brown ends. Bring two cups of water to a boil. Add the bundle of needles. Reduce heat and let simmer for 15 min.

Cranberry Tea (low bush)

4 handfuls of cranberries
1 handful of sugar (brown)

Cover ingredients with water, boil until cranberries are soft. Use a sieve and force the juice out of the cooked mix. Add sugar and or water to taste.

Cranberry Tea (high bush)

Same as above, but use a bit more sugar. It tastes better than it smells.

Possum Grape Drink

Use only those that are still sour after frost.   Gather ripe possum grapes. Hang up for winter use. To prepare, shell off the grapes from the stems, wash, stew in water. Let this sit until the seeds settle. Strain off the juice. Bring juice to a boil and thicken with a little cornmeal. Keep cooking until meal is done.

Wild Grape Drink

Put grapes in a kettle and cover with water. Mash the grapes. Bring to a boil, and let simmer for about 15 min. Cool, strain, and add maple sugar. to taste (table sugar may be used).

Maple Sugar Drink

Add as much maple sugar to cold water as will dissolve.

Molasses Milk Drink

1 T. thick molasses
1 C. cold milk

cinnamon (dash)

Combine all of above. Shake well.

Molasses Egg Nog

1 egg separated
2 tsp. molasses
nutmeg

1 C. cold milk
salt

Beat egg yolk, add molasses; mix well. Add milk, salt and a few grains of nutmeg. Beat egg whites stiff. Fold in.

Sassafras Tea

Gather and wash the roots of the red sassafras. Do this in early spring before the sap rises. Store for future use. To make tea, boil a few of the pieces of roots. Serve hot. Sweeten if desired. The boiled roots may be used again until the strength is gone.

Peppermint Tea

Gather peppermint, the kind that grows along the branches. Crush the leaves, pour boiling water over them, and serve hot. Sweeten to taste.

Hominy Corn Drink

Shell corn, soak in lye until the skin can be taken off. Beat corn in beater until the size of hominy. Sift meal from the husk particles. Cook corn particles until done. Drink hot or cold.

Labrador Tea

Dry leaves of the labrador plant, add two handfuls of dried leaves to about eight cups of boiling water. Reduce heat and let simmer about 10 min.

Desserts

Molasses Bread Pudding

6 slices of bread cubes　　　　*3 T. sugar*
2 eggs　　　　　　　　　　　*3 T. molasses*
salt　　　　　　　　　　　　*2 C. scalded milk*
2 T. butter, melted

Put bread cubes in well greased baking dish Beat eggs, molasses, sugar and salt together. Add milk and butter. Pour over bread cubes. Put in pan of hot water and bake 350° oven for 1 hour or until firm.

Huckleberry Pie

1 C. sugar
2 C. berries

Pour this mix on pie crust then cover with top crust. Bake at 450° for 15 min. or until brown.

Dried Apples

Peel and quarter ripe apples, or slice and dry them in the sun. Cook the dried apples until done. If they need thickening, add corn meal and cook 'til done. These make good fried pies.

Pudding

1 qt. milk
1/2 C. molasses
2 eggs
1 C. cold milk

1 tsp.
5 tsp. cornmeal
I tsp. ginger

Scald milk in double boiler. To the hot milk, add gradually the cornmeal.
Cook 15 min., stir constantly. Add molasses, salt, ginger, and well beaten
eggs. Pour into buttered baking dish. Put dish in pan of hot water, and
bake 2 hr. in moderate oven. Stir now and then. Serve hot or cold.

Persimmon Pudding

1 3/4 C. buttermilk
1/4 lb. butter
2 C. flour
2 C. persimmons

2 eggs
2 C. sugar

Press enough persimmons through a colander to make 2 cups. In another bowl, beat eggs, add milk, sugar, and melted butter. Then add the flour and persimmons. Mix well, pour into 9x12 baking dish. Bake at 400 'til even brown.

Rhubarb Pie

2 C. cooked and cooled rhubarb
2 egg yolks
1 T. cornstarch

1/2 C. milk
1 C. sugar

Mix above and stir well. Put in unbaked pie shell, dot with butter and bake 'til firm. Top with egg whites beaten stiff with 1/4 C. sugar. Brown in oven. Bake at 350°.

Dried Berries

Dry in the sun or by fire. Use as a flavoring agent such as wild rice, soup, bread, etc.

Cooked Berries

Put cleaned berries in a pot, as an equal amount of maple sugar, then, cover with water. Should be cooked to taste.

Deep Dish Apple Crisp

Peel and slice good firm and tart apples. Put slices in large pie plate until it is full. For topping, beat two eggs and 1 C. sugar together, add 2 tsp. melted butter. Beat well.

Fold in 1 C. sifted flour with 1 tsp. baking powder and 1/2 tsp. salt. Add 1 tsp. baking powder, and 1/2 tsp. salt. Add 1 tsp. vanilla. Spread mix over apples and bake at 350° until the apples are done and the top is crisp. This will be about 45 min.

Baked Apples

Pick ripe apples. Cover with hot ashes and live coals. Cook until soft.

Berries Preserved in Fat

Use equal weights of deer tallow and berries. Warm until soft and pliable so the berries can be worked into the fat. Keep in a cool place

Fried Apple Rings

Cut tart apple in rings about 1/2 inch wide. Remove core. Sprinkle both sides with 2 T. sugar. Cook in 1/8 inch hot fat on low heat until tender and glazed (about 5 min.).

Relishes

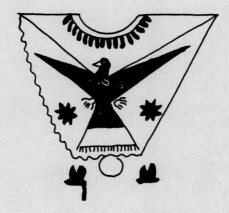

Green Tomato Pickle

Chop peck of tomatoes, 3 onions, 1/4 pint of horseradish, 3 green peppers. Drain all this dry. Salt in layers and let stand overnight. Drain. Scald vinegar and pour over it. Let stand 3 days, drain. Mix qt. of vinegar, 1 T. black pepper, one T. of allspice, 3 oz. ground cloves, 3 oz. dry mustard, and 1/4 pint of mustard seed. Bring to boil. Pour over pickles and let stand.

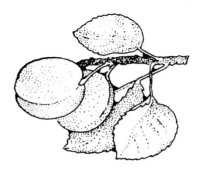

Pickled Peaches

One pint cooked peach halves. To the syrup add 3/4 C. firmly packed brown sugar, 1/2 C. vinegar, two 3" sticks of cinnamon, 1 tsp. whole cloves, 1 tsp. allspice.

Boil 5 min. Add the peach halves and simmer for another 5 min. Chill in the syrup several hours or overnight. Excellent with meats.

Apple Relish

Grind 2 med. hot peppers and 5 minced onions. Add 1 T. salt. Add 1 C. boiling water. Let stand 15 min., drain. Add 12 large apples that have been chopped with skins on, but that have had cores removed. Mix 1 qt. vinegar, 1 C. sugar, and add the following that have been put in cloth bag: 1 T. whole Spice, 1 T. cloves, and 1 stick of cinnamon.

Cook all this together for 15 min. Take bag of spices out, and discard.

Easy Dill Pickles

1 grape leaf
1 clove garlic
1 hot pepper

1 rib celery, but small
1 head of dill

Put all in qt. jar. Fill rest of jar with sliced cucumbers. In saucepan, combine 2 qt. water, and 1 qt. vinegar, 3/4 C. salt. Boil 5 min. Pour over the cucumbers, and seal. Let stand 15 days.

Pickled Beans

Mix 2/3 lemon juice, 1/2 C. oil, 2 tsp. salt, pepper to taste, 1 tsp. dry mustard, 1/2 C. pearl onions. Add to 1 lb. green beans that have been slightly cooked. Put in a crock. Let stand 4 days, covered.

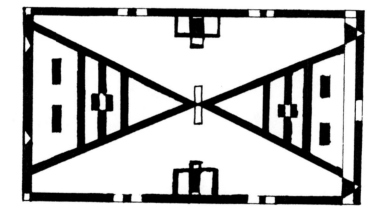

Soups

Snapping Turtle Soup

Remove head and claws. Remove the bottom shell. Remove and skin the legs, and neck meat. Cut meat into small pieces, cover with water and simmer 'til tender. Cook vegetables with the meat.

Spring Soup

1 med. onion
1 med. potato
3/4 tsp. salt
1 can 6 oz. tomato paste
1 1/2 C. chicken broth
2 T. raw rice

1 C. cut water cress,
  firmly pressed
1 T. butter
1 sliced carrot
1 C. water

Cook onion slowly in butter until browned slightly. Add all but water cress. Simmer, stirring occasionally, for 45 min. Add water cress and boil 5 min. longer.   A piece of watercress makes a nice garnish. Goes well with venison.

Sunflower Seed Soup

2 C. shelled sunflower seeds   *6 C. water*
3 scallion, sliced   *chicken broth to taste*
1 tsp. salt

Simmer all for 45 minutes

Hominy Soup

Put wood ashes lye into a pot, add water, and bring to a boil. Add corn, and stir until grain turns yellow. Pour into sieve basket to remove excess lye.

Pound grains in corn beater, until all grains are cracked several times. Sieve this cracked corn to get rid of bran. Winnowing in flat baskets works well. Put grits left from sieving into boiling water. Cook briskly 'til soft.

Noodles

1 egg
1/2 C. flour
1/4 tsp. salt

Beat egg with flour and salt. Work 'til smooth. Put on well floured dough board. Roll cut with pin until very, very thin. Cut into 4 inches strips, flour, and put on top of each other after they have laid out in warm air near fire, and have become dry and stiff.

Slice the stack of strips in 1/8 inch by 4 inch strips. Very dry before use. Dust with flour. Later drop these into venison or chicken broth, (beef can be used) cook 25 min. Add butter to taste.

Meat Skin Soup

Boil any kind of meat skins until done. Bake or roast until brown. Put in kettle of water with salt and boil 'til flavor is right. Thicken with cornmeal. Cook until cornmeal is done.

Turtle Soup

1 1/2 lb. turtle meat	1 T. flour
1 T. Crisco	small onion
1 can tomato sauce	stock in which turtle was
2 boiled eggs	cooked
1 tsp. ground clove	1 tsp. cinnamon
1/2 tsp nutmeg	1 glass fruit juice
1/2 sliced lemon	

Clean and cut turtle in small pieces. Boil in water (salted) until very tender. Cut in smaller pieces. Brown flour over low heat in the Crisco and add chopped onion and brown.

Mash two hard cooked egg yolks with cloves, cinnamon, and nutmeg. Blend well and pour into the tomato sauce. Then pour this into pot containing meat and stock. Boil about 40 min., simmer 20 min. along with fruit juice, lemon and a bit of garlic. Add cooked whites of egg sliced thin. Season again to taste.

Fish Soup

Clean and bake fish very brown. Put into pot of water and cook until done. Serve with main dish.

Hickory Nut Soup

Gather hickory nuts or scaly barks and dry on a rack before the fire. When nuts are dry, crack them by using a large flat rock put in a flat basket lined with cloth. Use smaller rocks to pound the nuts on the large rock. When nuts are cracked, sieve them through sieve basket.

Put kernels and small hulls that go through sieve in the corn beater and pound until it can be made into balls. Roll into balls until ready to use. Ball will keep several days if weather is not too warm.

Put balls in container, pour boiling water over them, and stir constantly.

Potato Soup

Peel white potatoes and cut them into small pieces.   Boil in water with onion until potatoes and onion smash easily. After smashing, add some fresh milk, and reheat mix. Season if desired.

Egg Soup

Beat bird eggs slightly and pour into boiling water. Season with salt and grease. Add meat if desired.

Corn & Bear Jerky Soup

3 oz. diced jerky
2 T. butter (margarine can
  be substituted)
2 C. stone-mashed green corn
  (1 can cream style corn can
  be substituted)

pinch of salt
1/2 C. chopped onions
3 diced potatoes
1 C. milk

Saute onion in butter. Combine bear jerky, onion and potatoes and cook until potatoes are tender. Stir in corn, milk and salt.

Bean Soup

2 C. dried shelled beans
1 slice raccoon cold meat
1 onion (cut up)
1 stalk celery, diced
1 finely ground carrot
1/4 T. dry mustard

pepper
1 C. pepper Ka-So-Ru (can
  substitute 1 T. Worcestersauce
  sauce)
salt if desired

Cover the beans with water and soak several hours or overnight. Add enough water to cover and add rest of ingredients. Cook until beans are entirely mush.

Prairie Dog/Cabbage Soup

1 lb. ground prairie dog meat
salt and pepper to taste
1/2 C. chopped onion
1/2 C. chopped celery

1 lb. boiled tomatoes
2 C. shredded cabbage
1 lb. soaked dry beans

Brown prairie dog meat and onion. Mix with other ingredients and heat until vegetables are tender but crisp.

Ghost Dance Soup

2 lb. ground bear meat
1 1/2 tsp. salt
5 C. water
2 large potatoes (cubed)

1 chopped onion
1 pt. tomato juice
1/3 C. sugar

Brown bear meat in skillet; drain. Add meat and water, salt, and onion. Cook over low heat about 30 min. Add tomato juice, sugar, and potatoes. Simmer until potatoes are cooked.

Corn Soup

8 slices of bacon
1 large diced onion
1 qt. water
4 C. diced, peeled potatoes
3 C. mashed green corn
 (can substitute 2 cans of
 cream style corn)

1 qt. milk or 1 pt. light cream
3 tsp salt
1/2 tsp seasoned pepper
2 T. butter (can substitute
 margarine)

In a 5 qt. dutch oven, cook the bacon until crisp, remove bacon, drain, then cool until needed. Discard all but 2 T. of bacon drippings, add onion to drippings and saute 'til soft. Add water, potatoes, and corn. Cover and simmer for 20 min. Add milk and season. Cool. Reheat slowly, stirring constantly, add butter. Crumble bacon and recrisp. Put uncovered in 350° oven until hot. Sprinkle over soup. Makes 8 servings.

Clam Chowder

double handful of minced clams
1 1/2 C. milk
1 1/2 tsp. salt
1/4 lb diced pork or 3-4 strips of bacon
 (do not use grease)

5 medium potatoes (sliced)
2 C. water
1/2 C. cream
dash of pepper

Fry bacon. Mix water, potatoes, onion and liquid from clams. Put in pan and cook until potatoes are tender (10-15 min.). Add milk, cream, clams, salt, pork or bacon. Heat until it reaches boiling stage. (Do Not Boil!!) Season with butter to taste.

Clam Chowder Soup

1/4 C. diced bacon
1/4 C. chopped onion
double handful of clams
  minced or whole clams
  (drained, reserve liquid)
2 C. pared, diced potatoes
1 C. water

1/3 C. celery
1 (16 oz.) can tomatoes
1 tsp. snipped parsley
1 tsp. salt
1/4 tsp. thyme
1/8 tsp. pepper

In large saucepan cook and stir bacon and onion until bacon is crisp and onion tender. Stir in potatoes, water, celery. Cook uncovered until potatoes are tender, about 10 min. Add clams, tomatoes and seasonings. Heat to boiling.

Sweet Spreads
for Breads

Peach-Plum

Wash, peel, and pit 4 C. of peaches, and 5 C. of plums. Cut fruit into small pieces. Put in large kettle. Add 8 C. sugar and one thinly sliced onion and stir well. Boil fast, stirring all the time until jellying is reached, or it becomes very thick. Take from heat, skim and stir for 5 min. Ladle into hot jar.

Sassafras Jelly

Put 2 C. of strong sassafras tea in a pan. Add pectin. Bring to slight boil. Add 3 C. strained honey, and 2 T. of sassafras root bark grated to fine powder. Simmer 6 min. Put in hot jelly glasses, cover.

73

Corn Cob Jelly

Boil a dozen red corn cobs in 3 pints of water. Do this for 30 min. Take from heat and strain. Bring up to 3 cups with water. Add fruit pectin, and bring to boil. Add 3 C. sugar, and boil 2-3 min., until jelly stage. Is beautiful apple jelly color.

Apple Butter

Cook 8 cups of apples, 5 cups of sugar, 1/2 cup of vinegar slowly for 30 minutes. For a modern touch, add 1/2 pound of red cinnamon candy. Put in hot sterile jars, and seal.

Apple Butter

16 C. cooked apple pulp   *juice of 1 lemon*
8 C. sugar   *4 tsp. cinnamon*

Put on heat and cook gently, stirring as necessary. Cook until the pulp is thick and the top is glossy. Optional: Color with flower blossoms crushed for their color.

Fruit Honey

4 C. wild bee honey   *1 C. ripe berry pulp*

Warm the honey in the sun, or on a low fire until it is thin enough to stir well. Add the berry pulp, and stir until well mixed.

Strawberry or Raspberry Jam

1 C. crushed berries   *2 C. sugar*

Boil for seven minutes.

Breads

Acorn Bread

Grind acorn meats that are well dried. Grind fine enough to be a flour. Add water to make the dough. Bake on a flat rock by the fire. Rock should be turned to get even heating.

Cracklin' Bread

2 C. cornmeal   *1 C. cracklings*
1 T. Salt

Add enough hot water to make into thick dough to form into small loaves. Cracklings should be in small pieces and as free of fat as possible. Bake in moderate oven for 45 min.

Gingerbread

1 C. shortening	1 C. sugar
1/2 C. black molasses	2 eggs
1/2 tsp. salt	1/4 tsp. soda
2 C. flour	1 tsp. baking powder
1 tsp. ginger	1 tsp. cinnamon

Mix all above. Add 1 cup boiling water, and stir. Bake at 300° for 45 min.

Mush

Add enough cornmeal to enough salted boiling water to make thick. Cook until meal is done and mushy. Serve with milk or butter. Can be sliced and fried when cooled and set up.

Gritted Bread

Pick corn that is just a bit past roasting ears. Grit this corn. Make the gritted meal into plain bread or mix with beans. Mix with a little grease and stir in milk, water, or bean soup. Bake in oven.

Baked Grits

Cook grits. Season with salt, pepper, and small amount of milk. Put in greased baking dish, top with grated cheese. Bake at 350° 'til done.

Cornmeal Strips

1 C. yellow cornmeal
1/4 C. grated cheese
4 C. water

1 1/2 t. salt
1/4 C. soft butter

Add meal gradually to salted boiling water, stirring all the time. Cook 20 min. Turn into a buttered 8 inch square pan and chill to firm. Cut into strips 1 in. by 2 in. Split each strip in half, spread with butter, and sprinkle with cheese. Put halves together again and butter the top, sprinkle again with cheese. Put on buttered sheet and bake at 400° for 15 min. or until brown.

Berry Beverages

Hot and cold drinks are made by adding the juice of almost any berry to water. Some of the most common ones are,

Blueberries	Chokecherries
Wild Blackberries	Pincherries
Raspberries	Wild Plums
Strawberries	

Maple sugar can also be used to sweeten the drinks.

Berry plant leaves also make good tea. Fresh young leaves work best. Rose bush leaves also make a good tea.

Rose Hip Tea

Pick the hips after the first frost, then they are bright red. Wash, and remove the brushes. Add a few mint leaves. Bring to a boil, and let simmer 15 min.

Squash the hips, forcing out the juice. Strain, and add hot water to taste.

Chestnut Stuffing

1 qt. chestnuts
2 T. butter
1/4 C. bread

2 T. cream
salt and pepper to taste

Shell and blanch chestnuts and cook in boiling water 'til tender. Rub them through a sieve while still hot. Add rest of ingredients.
For blanching: With a knife, score an X on the flat side of each chestnut. In medium saucepan, cover them with water, heat to boiling for 1 min. Remove from heat and with a slotted spoon, remove 3-4 chestnuts at a time. Shell and skin, then coarsely chop nuts, set aside.

Walnut Meal

Crack the dry walnuts, and remove the meats. Beat them into a meal. This meal can be added to mealed corn or beans to suit the taste of the cook. The mixture is then cooked until it is thickened, then baked.

Fried Bread

Make a soft dough from 1 C. flour, baking powder, pinch of salt and some grease. Add enough milk to mix. Mix. Drop by spoonfuls into hot grease. Let fry to brown and crisp.

Salt Rising Bread

First Sponge:
1 C. milk
1 tsp. salt

2 T. cornmeal
2 T. sugar

Second Sponge:
1 C. of water (lukewarm)
1 T. sugar
2 C. sifted flour

pinch salt
2 T. shortening

Dough:
2 1/4 C. sifted flour

Scald the milk, bring down to room temperature, add cornmeal, salt, and sugar. Pour into bowl, cover and put in warm place. Let rest for 6 hrs. Add second sponge. Mix again. Cover and put in pan of water at 120°. Let rise until light. Add rest of flour until it is stiff enough to knead. Knead for 15 minutes. Shape into loaves, and put in greased pan.

Brush tops with melted butter or shortening. Cover, and let stand until it more than doubles in size. Bake at 375° for ten minutes, lower the heat to 350°, and bake 25-30 min. longer.

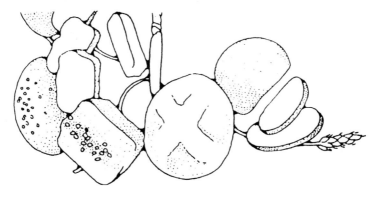

Cornbread Turkey Stuffing

1 qt. of old cornbread
  (broken to 1/2 inch)
3/4 C. diced celery
3 T. dried parsley
1/2 tsp. salt

1/3 C. fat
2 T. onion
pepper to taste

Use fat from chicken or turkey, add celery, parsley, and onion. Heat. Add cornbread. Mix well, but lightly. Bake 2 hr. at 350°.

Ash Cake

2 C. cornmeal
3/4 tsp. soda
salt to taste

1 C. buttermilk
1/3 C. fat

Add enough water to make a thick dough when mixed above. Make a hole in center of ashes of bonfire. Put dough in the hole. Let it crust and then cover with hot ashes. Bake to suit.

Crusty Bread

1/2 stick butter
1 tsp. baking powder
1 C. cold milk
1 egg

1 C. cornmeal
1 T. flour
2 tsp sugar
pinch of salt

Put 1/2 stick of butter in 9x5 pan. Put in preheated oven and melt butter. Do not burn. Mix flour, baking powder, salt and sugar. Add cold milk and egg. Beat for 1 min. Put in hot pan of butter. Bake 25-30 min.

Corn Bread

Let corn dry while still on the cob. Scrape the kernels off. Grind or mash until it is like a very coarse flour. Make a dough with water, and bake on a flat rock near the fire.

Creatures

Squirrel Stew

1 squirrel	*3 chunked potatoes*
1 small can tomatoes	*1 C. whole grain corn*
1 lg. onion, chopped	*salt*
small fist full of jerky	*pepper*
1 qt. water	*3 slices of bacon*

Put squirrel in pan. Chunk the bacon, and add, along with the water. Simmer until the squirrel is tender, then add the rest of ingredients. Season to taste. Allow to stew until the potatoes are tender.

Baked Prairie Chicken

2 Prairie Chickens	*butter*
6 slices bacon	*3/4 C. water*
1 T. flour	

Salt and pepper each chicken both on the outside and the inside. Wrap bacon around the chickens. Put in dish well-greased with the butter. Bake in dish, breast side down for 10 min. at 450°. Then for 30 min. at 325°. Baste as necessary to keep moist.

Stir Fry Buffalo

1 1/2 lb. strip meat	1 T. finely ground corn
1/4 C. oil	1/4 C. soy sauce
1 onion, sliced	1 C. tomato sauce
1 1/2 C. celery, sliced	1 tsp. sugar
3/4 C. carrots, sliced	1/4 tsp. ground ginger
1 green pepper	3 C. cooked rice

Strips should be about 2 inches long, and very thin. Sear meat, add onion rings, celery, and carrots. Stir and fry to crisp-tender. Blend ground corn in soy sauce and stir in tomato sauce, and seasonings. Add all to skillet with green pepper. Stir and fry 3-5 min. more 'til sauce thickens and becomes shiny. Serve on hot rice.

Roast Duck

2 ducks	1 small onion
1/2 C. vinegar	1 slivered orange rind
1/2 C. broth	salt and pepper to taste

Dampen ducks and season with salt and pepper. Slice onion and place against the ducks and on top. Put ducks and all other ingredients in pan, and into oven preheated to 450°. Roast for 15-20 min., depending on size of ducks. Baste with drippings.

Pheasant Casserole

1 Pheasant	*4 C. milk*
1/2 C. melted butter	*1 tsp. salt*
bacon grease	*1/2 tsp. pepper*
1/2 C. flour	*1 tsp. sage*

Mix the salt, pepper, and sage, and roll pieces of pheasant in the mixture. Brown in bacon grease in separate pan, mix butter, milk and 6 T. flour, stir and bring to boil. Pour mix over the pheasant that had been put in a baking dish with bacon laid over it. Bake until tender.

Venison Stew

2-3 lb. venison	*3 T. bacon fat*
6 potatoes	*bay leaf*
6 carrots	*salt*
cabbage	*pepper*
3 onions	*hot water*

Chop all vegetables coarsely. Using bacon fat, brown cubed meat. Add the hot water to cover the meat. Simmer one hour; add carrots, salt and pepper, and the bay leaf. Let simmer 30 min. Add potatoes and onions. Cook 30 min., then add seasonings and water as needed.

Buffalo Brisket

1 brisket
1 C. oil
3 T. soy sauce
1 clove garlic, smashed

1 tsp. liquid smoke
1 T. salt
1 C. water

Marinate overnight. Bake at 250° for 5-6 hrs. Add 1 C. of water just before baking. Slice brisket thinly, and serve with gravy from marinate.

Weasel Meatroll

1 1/2 lb. deboned weasel
1 egg
3/4 C. small hunks dry bread
1/2 C. onion
1 pt. tomato sauce

1 tsp. salt
1/2 tsp.oregano
1/8 tsp. pepper
2 C. cheese

Mix meat, egg, bread, onion, 1/4 of tomato sauce, salt, oregano, and pepper. Mix and shape into flat rectangle (10x12). Sprinkle cheese over. Roll up, and press ends to seal. Bake in shallow dish at 350° 1 hr. Drain off excess fat, add rest of tomato sauce, and bake 15 min. more.

Venison Stones of Meat
(meatballs)

1 lb. venison (ground)
1 egg
1 tsp. salt
2 C tomato juice

dash of pepper
1 chopped onion
1 C. crushed corn
  kernels
(1 1/2 C. cornflakes can
  be substituted)

For balls. Brown in hot fat, and put in dish. Cover with tomato juice. Be sure the balls are completely covered. Bake 350° for 45 min. Add water if necessary to keep balls covered.

Raccoon Meatballs

1 lb. ground raccoon meat
1/4 C. dry bread crumbs
1 tsp. salt
1 C. grape jelly

1 egg, beaten
1 C 50/50 red pepper
  and water, crushed
  and mixed.

Add meat, crumbs, salt and egg. Shape into balls the size of walnut shells. Brown. Add pepper/water, and jelly. Simmer. Serve warm.

Elk Meatballs

1 lb. ground elk meat
1 C. dry bread crumbs
1/2 C. cheese
1/8 tsp. celery salt
1 T. minced parsley
1 clove garlic (minced)
1/2 C. milk.

1/2 C. milk
2 eggs (beaten)
salt
pepper
1 can cream of mushroom
  soup

Mix all ingredients and shape into walnut-sized balls. Cover meatballs with a mix of one can cream of mushroom soup and 1/2 C. milk. Simmer about 30 min., or can be cooked in slow cooker 4 hours.

Stone Mealed Apples Meatloaf

2 lb. of venison, beef or buffalo
3/4 C. stone mealed apple
   (modern cooks can use apple
   sauce)
2 tsp. salt

2 eggs
2 tsp. chopped onion
1/2 C. milk

Combine and mix. Form an indent on top. Cover with a sauce made from
1/4 C. catsup
2 T. brown sugar
1 tsp. prepared mustard

Venison Meat Loaf

1/2 lb. ground venison
1 3/4 C. bread crumbs
1 1/2 tsp. salt
1 1/2 tsp. grated lemon
1 beaten egg
pepper

3 T. butter
3 T celery
1 C. water
1 bay leaf
1/4 tsp. marjoram

Saute celery in butter. Add bay leaf and water. Let simmer for 3 min.
Throw away bay leaf, cool. Add bread crumbs. Add venison and rest of
ingredients. Mix. Form into a loaf, and bake 1 hr. at 350°.

Oven Fried Deer Steak

1 tsp. salt
1 tsp. soda
4 T. vinegar
water to cover

1 can mushroom soup
1 can water
Deer steak (for 4)

Soak deer steak in salt, soda, and vinegar with enough water to cover the meat for 4-5 hr. Drain meat. Tenderize with a hammer. Salt, pepper and flour the meat. Brown in a skillet. Put in baking dish. Pour in mushroom soup and can of water. Bake at 350° until tender (about 45 min.).

Potato and Venison

1 lb. venison
1/3 C. chopped onions
1/3 C. chopped green pepper
1 T. catsup

1 can cream of mushroom
  soup
1/4 C. water
2 med. potatoes cubed

Combine venison, onion, pepper in skillet. Cover, heat over medium heat until heat is browned and onions and pepper is tender. Add catsup, soup, and water. Put into casserole and cover with potato cubes. Bake uncovered at 350° for 35 min.

Fish Head Broth

Cover in pot with an inch of water. Add wild onions, dill, ginger, or fat. Simmer, strain, and serve hot.

Locusts

Gather the locusts (cicada) at night. Put them out of shell. Do not let the sun shine on them, or they will spoil. Wash and fry locust in small amount of grease. Eat hot or cold.

Pheasant

Dress pheasant, put on a stick before the fire or over coals and roast 'til brown. Put browned pheasant in pot of water and boil 'til well done. Thicken soup with cornmeal and season with salt.

Squirrel of the Sky (Birds)

Clean bird, and leave as whole as possible. Run stick through it and roast before the fire. Serve with mush.

Baked Fish

Put layer of clay over the whole fish. Then build fire. When good hot coals are ready, dig hole in ground, cover with more clay, and put hot coals on top. Leave about 2 hours. Modern cooks might want to gut the fish, and wrap it in foil so dirt does not get into the fish before doing this.

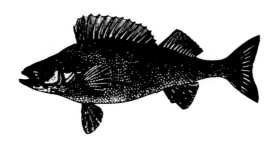

Quail on Toast

6 Quails
1 T. butter
6 slices homemade bread,
  toasted

sliced lemon
1 T. water
parsley
6 slices bacon

Pick, singe, clean, and wipe the quails. Butter inside of each and sprinkle with salt and pepper. Rub butter on outside and wrap a thin slice of bacon around each quail.

Melt butter in pan. Add birds, cook in oven 20-30 min., and put bird on hot buttered toast. Add a little butter, T. water, and the lemon juice. Strain and pour over breasts of birds. Garnish with parsley.

Fish Soup

Chunks of fish and any vegetables put in cold water. Seasonings added, then boil water. Immediately cut down on heat so it only simmers. Cook until fish falls off bones.

Boiled Roe

Cook in water, but do not let it come to a rolling boil. Add lemon juice to water. Season as desired.

Raccoon

Clean the raccoon. Par-boil in water with red pepper added. When tender, take from pot, add salt and pepper. Bake in oven 'til brown.

Boiled or Fried Roe

Boil in water or fry in animal fat. Add maple sugar by sprinkling on just before serving.

Boiled Whitefish

Clean and scale, then cut into chunks. Put in cold water, add seasonings to taste. Add salt pork if desired. Boil then simmer until flakes off bone easily.

Smoked Fish Soup

Smoked and deboned fish are cut into bite-sized pieces. Add water. Vegetable greens can be added just after water comes to boil. Reduce heat to soup, simmering about 12-15 min. Season as desired.

Bullfrogs

Cut legs off at hip, and remove feet. Peel off the skin. Fry or boil.

Frogs

Catch them early in morning. Twist off heads, peel off skin while holding under running water. Par-boil and then cook like any other meat.

Prairie Fire Mouth

*1 lb. ground venison
  (beef may be used)
salt and pepper to taste
Red kidney beans
  (modern cooks use 2 cans)*

*1 T. chili powder
2 cans tomatoes
1/2 tsp. sugar
1 onion*

Cook onion in 2 T. fat. Add venison and stir all the time until separated well. Add tomatoes, salt and pepper. Cook until tomatoes are cooked to pieces, and mix is thick. Add chili powder, and beans. Let simmer for a time. Serve with cheese, pickles, and crackers.

Freshwater Clams

Open clam with heavy knife. Cut muscle away from shell. The neck and other parts should be discarded. Can be boiled, broiled, or fried.

Knee Deeps (Frogs)

Catch frogs. Scald them, skin, and par-broil. Cook them like other meat.

Venison (or Beef) Hot Dish

*sliced potatoes (very thin)
sliced onion
sliced green pepper
tomato juice*

*1/2 C. dry rice
2 lb. Venison (beef)
  browned in skillet*

Layer in baking dish, season each layer. Bake one hour, covered.

Opossum

Cook just the ground hog. Do not eat very much opossum at one time.

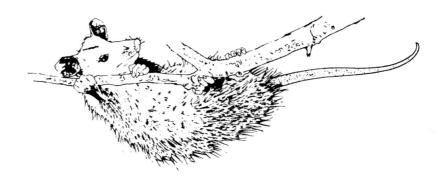

Groundhog

Get a fat groundhog, and clean. Par-boil until tender. Sprinkle with salt, pepper, and red pepper. Bake before fire or in oven.

Yellow Jacket and Comb Soup

Gather yellow jackets from nest in ground. Place over heat right side up to loosen grubs. Remove grubs. Put comb over heat again until outside parches. Remove and pick out yellow jackets and brown them in oven. Make soup by boiling yellowjackets in water with seasoning, grease and salt.

Quail

Dress bird. Put on a stick before the fire or oven, not coals and leave til real brown. Put bird in pot of water, and boil 'til well done. Thicken soup with cornmeal. Season with salt.

Baked Squirrel

Dress fresh squirrel. Put in fire to singe. If cooking modern, a rolled up newspaper can be used. This should be done outside. Be careful not to set your clothes on fire!

Wash off singed hair and ashes. Wash again and remove innards. Rub inside and outside with lard. Bake before an open fire or in oven until brown.

Rabbit or Squirrel

Soak overnight in salted water (half vinegar). Stew or fry like chicken.

Fish Liver

Prepare as you would any beef liver.

Roast Turkey

Preheat oven to 325°, make stuffing. Remove giblets from med. turkey. Clean turkey, stuff neck cavity. Tuck skin flap back over stuffing. Cut off tough wing tips.

Boil drumsticks since they take longer to cook. Butter and baste turkey occasionally with pan drippings. When golden brown, cover with husks (or aluminum foil). Drippings make good gravy.

Venison Roast

Pick medium boneless roast. Slit sides and top at 3 inch intervals, and stuff with pieces of chopped onion, bay leaf, salt and pepper, ground cloves, and allspice. Pour vinegar to cover meat, leave in covered dish 12 hr. or more.

To cook, coat meat with lard and flour, and brown quickly. Pour in the same vinegar, cover, and cook 20 minutes per pound. Slice and serve hot or cold.

Rabbit

2 young rabbits
2 tomatoes
1 bay leaf
1 qt. beef stock
pepper
Whole spice

1 minced onion
  (chives can be used)
2 T. flour
sprig of thyme
salt
green pepper

Clean and cut rabbit into pieces. Let stand overnight in vinegar and onions, thyme, parsley, whole spice, salt and pepper and green or hot pepper. When ready to fix rabbit, take from liquid, rinse and dry. Then fry. Brown onion in flour, then add tomatoes. Let smother well before adding hot stock. Let come to boil, and simmer for 1 hour in all other seasoning.

Bird on Toast

Clean and split birds down the back to make four pieces. Salt and pepper and rub with butter and apple juice. Pin on thin slice of bacon with small stick, and put in roaster. Broil on both sides in oven. Serve on buttered toast with fat fried potatoes and a green salad.

Small Fish

String on a green stick, and hold over fire. Cook slowly, turning often.

Large Fish

Cut along the backbone, put on a spit (greenwood) and punch other end in ground. Cook slowly.

Barbecued Fish

Cut fish into strips or chunks, string on pieces of sharpened sticks. Hang over fire. Turn often. Heat until no longer drips. Hang on thongs of leather or grass.

Dried Fish

Split fish (except the very small ones) and open for better drying. Dry near fire, turning for even drying. Cut up the dried fish, and make a soup from them.

Bird and Mushroom Casserole

Cut up the dressed bird as you would if you were going to fry it. Salt and pepper should be sprinkled on, and the pieces rolled in flour. Brown over medium heat. Put in casserole dish, and cover with mushroom soup, cut half and half with water. Bake for 1 1/2 hour in oven pre-heated to 300°.

Broiled Birds

Either dress or skin. Barbecue over hot coals on a spit. Can be basted with butter or sauce if desired, but not necessary. Best done with young tender birds.

Eggs

Simply cook in boiling water, break open and eat.

Stewed Birds

Either dress or skin. Then boil in pot with potatoes or wild rice. When the meat falls off the bone, it is ready.

Pickled Tongue

1 pt. vinegar	*1 pt. water*
2 T. sugar	*1 tsp. whole cloves*
1 tsp. whole allspice	*1 tsp. whole black pepper*
1/2 tsp. mustard seed	*1/2 tsp.salt*

Wash tongue in salted water, then put in fresh water. Add 1 tsp. of allspice, and simmer 1-2 hr. or to tender. Cool, peel off skin and cut off roots. Submerge in pickling solution made from above that has been boiled for 10 min. Refrigerate, and age one week.

Duck Soup

Clean duck, and twist a wire around the neck skin so no liquid can escape. Hang in smoke house, head down, and fill body with can of soup. Smoke the duck until done (8-10 hr.). Some folks go ahead and eat the duck, but throw the soup away.

Broiled Caribou Heads

The de-antlered and skinned head is barbecued over coals 'til done. This can take a long time, even over a day.

Rendering of Animal Fat

Lard can be prepared from almost any animal fat. The best fat to use is that from the animal's back. Very often an animal will have rather large hunks of fat around the stomach.

Simply cut the fat into cubes of 3/4 to one inch square, and cooked in a kettle at a high heat.

Do not let the heat get high enough to make the lard smoke.

When the tissue seems to be free of any more fat, take the molten lard off by carefully pouring. Allow to cool. It will look nicer if stirred now and then while cooking.

Rabbit

2 rabbits, dressed, and cleaned	*1/2 C. oil*
1 C. wine	*2 sliced onions*
1 T. allspice	*1 tsp. salt*
2 dashes of pepper	*1/4 C. flour*
2 T. sugar	

Cut the rabbit into pieces. Make a marinade of oil, wine, onion, allspice, salt and pepper. Cover meat, cover dish and cool. Marinate for 1 1/4 days. Drain. Dredge in seasoned flour and brown. Remove rabbit and pour off all liquids. Put in pan and cover with marinade. Add sugar. Boil, and then simmer to tender.

Bird and Wild Rice Casserole

1 C. wild rice
flour
1 deboned and pieced bird
1 chopped onion
1 chopped green pepper

jar pimentos
1 can mushroom soup
1 can of water
salt
pepper

Simmer the rice for one hour in 2 qt. water. Cut bird into chunks after deboning. Season, roll in flour and fry to brown, but not crusty. When almost done, add onion & pepper. Continue frying and add pimento, soup, and water. Bake at 300° for 1 1/2 hr. in greased casserole. Add water while baking.

Almost Hatched Ducks

Just before a duckling is to hatch, boil the egg to a hard boil. Remove and eat.

Baked Squirrel

2 *whole dressed squirrels*   1 *onion, sliced*
1 *onion, cut into quarters*   2 *slices bacon*
salt   *pepper*

Put onions in baking dish, put squirrels on top. Stuff the bodies with the onion. Alternate onions slices and bacon slices over the squirrel. Bake in covered dish at 350° until tender. Timing depends on age of squirrel. The younger ones will cook faster.

Heart

Clean the heart, cut it open to remove the arteries, veins, and fat. Make stuffing of 2 C. of dried bread pieces, 1/4 C. chopped celery, 1/4 C. chopped onion, and season to taste with salt and pepper. Add pats of butter as you stir the mix together.

Stuff the heart with the stuffing, close openings with skewers. Sprinkle the outside with salt and pepper. Roll in flour or cracker crumbs, and brown in oil. Bake at 325° for 1 1/2 hours.

Fried Skunk

Clean and dress. Marinate overnight in salt water with vinegar. Cool dry. Cut into chunks and fry in oil.

Roasted Skunk

Clean and dress. Marinate overnight in salt water with vinegar. Cool and dry. Roast in a covered pan, with onions.

Squaw Candy

Cut salmon into strips and allow to dry until chewy. This should be done in an oven at 150°.

Tongue

Use tongue of any large game animal. Simmer in water for one to two hours. Peel off the skin and cut off root ends. Slice and serve.

Beaver Tail Stew

Skin the tail, cut into chunks and use to make stew. Vegetables can be added as desired.

Beaver Tail

Skin the tail, cut into steaks and fry. The meat should be cut across the grain.

Salmon Eggs

Dry the eggs in the sun or in a drier. Fry in a little light oil, add salt.

Jerky

Cut meat into strips, remove all fat, and dry in 150° oven for five or six hours. Sponge off any remaining fat, and store in cool, dry place.

Kidneys

Remove the kidneys, and clean. Materials that are foreign to the kidney tissue should be removed. Such things would be skin or ducts. Gently boil for 30 min., change water and simmer for an additional 30 min. During the second simming, onions should be cut up and added to the water. The kidneys can then be cut into chunks and eaten, or put in soups.

Rabbits

Dress, broil over hot coals. You might want to drip or brush fat or sauce over the meat now and then. Broil until tender.

Rabbits

Dress, debone, cut into chunks, and fry. Flavor is much improved by tenderizing before frying. You might want to roll in flour or cracker crumbs before frying.

Raccoon

Skin, dress and revmove all fat. Be sure to remove the glands under each leg. They are in the shape of a bean. Broil over hot coals on a spit. The carcass can be heavy so be sure to use a stout green stick. Can be basted with butter or a barbecue sauce.

Jellied Moose Nose

Remove the nose and boil it for about 45 minutes. Cool it and remove the hair. Simmer the nose in water with 4 tsp. pickling spice, a bay leaf, and a chopped onion. Simmer until tender.

Remove from heat and allow to cool for several hours.

Remove the meat from the bone and cartilage. Cut the meat into slices and put into glass jar, then cover that with the liquid from the second boiling water. Cool so it will jell.

Large Animal Brains

Remove the brain, clean well, and simmer for 30-40 minutes. During the last ten minutes spices can be added. The spices can be allspice, mustard, or simply salt and pepper. After the simmering, the brains can be fried.

Porcupine Liver

Remove, clean, and fry in cooking oil. Can be tenderized by pounding with the edge of a plate, the back of a knife, or whatever. Some people prefer to roll in flour or cracker crumbs before frying.

Porcupine

Remove fat from the four "quarters," and soak in salt water with a couple tablespoons of vinegar for overnight. Drain and dry. Add salt and pepper. Dredge in flour, and brown in cooking oil. After browning, pour gravy or wine over the meat, then simmer until tender. Additional gravy or wine will need to be added as it boils down.

Large Animal Liver

Remove the liver, clean it well, and fry. Flour can be beat into the liver to make it more tender.

Raccoon

Skin, dress, and remove all fat. Roast in a roaster at 325° for about three hours. Test to see if tender from time to time since a larger raccoon will take longer to become tender. Any stuffing you would use for chicken can be used in roasting raccoon.

Tongue

Boil the tongue for one hour in water seasoned with bear grease, wild ginger, or dill. Cut the root end off, then peel the tongue. Slice and serve.

Medicine, Remedies, Beauty

Native American Remedies

It is easy for us to think that we brought medical practices to America from other parts of the world.

And. so we did. But, also, the Native Americans had their own medicines and their own practices.

Furthermore, modern medicine is increasingly finding that there is a lot more that superstition and wishful thinking to some of those old medicines.

Most of the medicines used by the American Indians were vegetable products...all sorts of leaves, seeds, roots, and tree barks.

Below is a list of some of the ailments to which humans fall heir, and products from the great outdoors that the Indians used to treat those ailments.

The reader is strongly urged to consider these treatments and medicines only for their historical interest. Neither the writer or the publisher of this book would want you to try these remedies, either in addition to traditional practices, or instead of traditional modern practices.

Blood problems	Sassafras
Jaundice	Black willow bark
Head colds	Ginger
Constipation	Bladder nut seeds
Hiccoughs	Tea of wild seeds
Snake bites	Slippery Elm bark
Bee stings	Mud from clay
Toothaches	Prickley ash bark
Sore Throat	Slippery Elm bark
Sore eyes	Yellow Root
Earaches	Tobacco smoke

Chills..Snake root
Warts...Milk of milkweed
Asthma..Leaves of mint
Backache..Tea of slippery elm

Beauty Aids

And, just like anyone else, the American Indians were interested in doing what they could to improve their appearance and to attract the opposite sex.

Some practices employed by the Plains Indians for various cosmetic purposes are as follows.

Again, the reader is urged not to try any of these. The writer and the publisher can offer no assurances whatsoever regarding their effectiveness or safety.

Clearness of skin....................................rubbing of the skin with the raw side of a freshly killed bird.

Silkiness and depth of color....................wash hair in a mixture of water of hair and the juice squeezed from the pulp of the wild plum.

Odor improvement..................................vigorous "bathing" in a fine clay dust that has been well warmed by the sun, then rinse in water.

Reversing of the process
of aging......................................swim in the dead of the night
when there is no moon
showing

Straightness of limbs.............................eating of at least a handful of
soil between the time of one
full moon, and the next.

Epilogue

So, be it locusts, pickled tongue, or beaver tail, the American Indians ate some things that seem pretty strange to many of us today.

But, some of their dishes are remarkably similiar to what the rest of us eat all the time. The American Indians had their potatoes, meatloaf, and even salads...much like we know.

So, again, as we look at another people, we find similarities that make us alike, and differences that make us interesting.

Notes of Explanation

A Problem

The author, in an attempt to do some authentic American Indian cooking made a careful study of the available cookbooks.

He found that the cookbooks he could find were all of two types. One kind was so authentic that he found them impossible to use. The ingredients were exotic and often unobtainable. It is nigh on to impossible, for example, for a cook, in these last years of the early years of the 21st 20th century to find many of the ingredients called for in recipes coming from way back in the latter part of the 19th century.

Your neighborhood grocer is probably fresh out of eel skins or a mix of otter fat and fermented flower-from-the-sky.

It is even more or a chore to lay one's hands on any Na-Yi-Neh-La, snal se-bana.

While these really authentic recipes might have the makings for some really fine eating, it doesn't make a difference if you can't get the ingredients together.

And the problem with the ingredients can be only part of the difficulty in trying to cook from those recipes.

Another serious problem is the measuring system. It isn't too hard to translate "a maiden's handful" to cups and a "squirrel skull measure" to teaspoons. But, how does one handle "half a stone corn grinder; or translate a length of bacon "a lodgepole thick" to inches?

Even such a simple thing as temperature of the oven. What temperature is "two hands' length from a small lodge fire" or "warm to make the dog run to the water."

Instructions from those cooks of so many years ago that speak of such things are instructions of almost no practical value.

On the other hand, so-called Indian recipes that call for a package of frozen mixed vegetables, or a box of instant cake mix certainly aren't really Indian recipes at all, but rather something that came off of a month-old cook's magazine.

Indian recipes that talk of microwave ovens and tater tots simply don't ring true.

What this writer has done is to work with translators and students of the Indian cultures in order to translate the original recipes into ingredients, measurements, and practices that modern cooks are used to.

You will find the eel skins have been changed to modern equivilants. Those exotic ingredients have been translated to modern ones, and "baked for a time to skin a buffalo" has been changed to "40 minutes".

Nothing translates perfectly, and attempts to change instructions from the language and practices of one culture to another can go sour.

But, this book is an attempt at that.

The adventurous cook is urged to give them a try. And, keep one ear tuned. You might well, as you put these dishes together, hear a distant thunder of hooves. You might hear the soft swish of an arrow, or some far off squeals of delight as some Indian children snag a turtle that will end up tonight in stew.

Need a Gift?

For

* Shower * Birthday * Mother's Day *
* Anniversary * Christmas *

Turn Page For Order Form
(Order Now While Supplies Last!)

Please send me _____ copies of *Indian Cooking* at $10.95 each plus $3.75 for the first book and $.75 for each additional copy for S/H.
(Make checks payable to Quixote Press.)

Name _____

Street _____

City _____ State ____ Zip _____

Hearts 'N Tummies Cookbook Co.
3544 Blakslee Street
Wever, IA 52658
1-800-571-2665

To Order Copies

Please send me _____ copies of *Indian Cooking* at $10.95 each plus $3.75 for the first book and $.75 for each additional copy for S/H.
(Make checks payable to Quixote Press.)

Name _____

Street _____

City _____ State ____ Zip _____

Hearts 'N Tummies Cookbook Co.
3544 Blakslee Street
Wever, IA 52658
1-800-571-2665